Supervision of U.S. Payment, Clearing, and Settlement Systems: Designation of Financial Market Utilities (FMUs)

Marc Labonte
Specialist in Macroeconomic Policy

September 10, 2012

Congressional Research Service
7-5700
www.crs.gov
R41529

CRS Report for Congress
Prepared for Members and Committees of Congress

Summary

The U.S. financial system processes millions of transactions each day representing daily transfers of trillions of dollars, securities, and other assets to facilitate purchases and payments. Concerns had been raised, even prior to the recent financial crisis, about the vulnerability of the U.S. financial system to infrastructure failure. These concerns about the "plumbing" of the financial system were heightened following the market disruptions of the recent crisis.

The financial market infrastructure consists of the various systems, networks, and technological processes that are necessary for conducting and completing financial transactions. Title VIII of the Dodd-Frank Act, P.L. 111-203, the *Payment, Clearing, and Settlement Supervision Act of 2010*, introduces the term "financial market utility" (FMU or utility) for those multilateral systems that transfer, clear, or settle payments, securities, or other financial transactions among financial institutions (FI) or between an FMU and a financial institution. Utilities and FIs transfer funds and settle accounts with other financial institutions to facilitate normal day-to-day transactions occurring in the U.S. economy. Those transfers include payroll and mortgage payments, foreign currency exchanges, purchases of U.S. treasury bonds and corporate securities, and derivatives trades. Further, financial institutions engage in commercial paper and securities repurchase agreements (repo) markets that contribute to liquidity in the U.S. economy. In the United States, some of the key payment, clearing, and settlement (PCS) systems are operated by the Federal Reserve, and other systems are operated by private sector organizations.

With Title VIII of the Dodd-Frank Act, which was enacted on July 21, 2010, Congress added a new regulatory framework for the FMUs and PCS activities (of FIs) designated by the Financial Stability Oversight Council as systemically important. On July 18, 2012, the Council voted unanimously to designate eight FMUs as systemically important. Title VIII expands the Federal Reserve's role, in coordination with those of other prudential regulators, in the supervision, examination, and rule enforcement with respect to those FMUs and PCS activities of financial institutions. Additionally, FMUs may borrow from the discount window of the Federal Reserve in certain unusual and exigent circumstances.

Although Title VIII primarily affects the scope of regulatory powers, certain provisions directly affect a utility's business operations. For example, Title VIII allows FMUs to maintain accounts at a Federal Reserve Bank and provides access to the Fed's discount window in unusual and exigent circumstances. Related to PCS, Title VII of the Dodd-Frank Act imposes requirements that will significantly affect the business of clearinghouses in the over-the-counter (OTC) derivatives (swaps) market. By requiring clearing of certain swap transactions through central counterparties (CCPs or clearinghouses), Title VII is expected to increase the volume of transactions processed by clearing systems subject to Title VIII.

Critics contend that Title VIII grants too much discretionary authority to the Fed in an area that they argue was not a source of systemic risk during the recent financial crisis. S. 3497 seeks to repeal Title VIII of the Dodd-Frank Act, stripping FSOC of it's authority to designate FMUs as systemically important.

This report outlines the changes to the supervision of key market infrastructure that are embodied in the Dodd-Frank Act. It is intended to be used as a reference for those interested in the financial system's "plumbing," and how the associated systems are currently overseen and regulated.

Contents

Introduction 1
Major Payment, Clearing, and Settlement Systems in the United States 3
    FMUs Designated by the FSOC 3
    Systems Operated by the Federal Reserve 4
Other Systems Operated by the Private Sector 5
Basics of Payment, Clearing, and Settlement 5
    Payment Systems 6
    Clearing Systems 7
    Settlement Systems 8
Risks of Payment, Clearing, and Settlement Systems and Activities 9
    Systemic Risk 10
    Other Risks 11
Regulatory Oversight Prior to Title VIII 12
    Recommendations to Strengthen Oversight 12
    Pre-Dodd-Frank Oversight 13
    Supervisory Policies 14
    International Regulatory Standards 15
Title VIII of the Dodd-Frank Act 16
    Exclusions 17
    FSOC Determines Systemic Importance 18
    Risk Management Standards 19
    Federal Reserve Services for Systemically Important Financial Market Utilities 20
    Examination and Enforcement 20
    Regulatory Coordination 21
Title VIII Implementation 22
    Financial Stability Oversight Council 22
    Federal Reserve 23
    CFTC and SEC 23
    Impact on Payment, Clearing, and Settlement Systems and Activities 24

Tables

Table A-1. Selected FMUs Designated Systematically Important by FSOC 25
Table A-2. Other PCS Systems 29

Appendixes

Appendix. Selected Payment, Clearing, and Settlement Systems in the United States 25

Contacts

Author Contact Information..32
Acknowledgments 33

Introduction

On July 21, 2010, Title VIII of the Dodd-Frank Act,[1] the *Payment, Clearing, and Settlement Supervision Act of 2010*, became effective upon enactment. Title VIII authorizes the Federal Reserve, in coordination with other federal agencies, to supervise and regulate the infrastructure that enables financial intermediaries to process and complete financial transactions.

Payment, clearing, and settlement (PCS) activities facilitate a variety of financial transactions such as transferring payments for and completing retail purchases, foreign exchange transactions, securities transactions, and derivatives trades. Some key systems in the United States have been operated by the Federal Reserve Banks and others by the private sector. PCS systems serve a critical role in the financial services sector and the broader economy. In the United States, the value of transactions for large-value payment systems amounted to $1.06 quadrillion in 2011.[2]

Attention was drawn to the functioning of the U.S. financial system in 2008 when major financial institutions entered bankruptcy (e.g., Lehman Brothers), receivership (e.g., Washington Mutual), or were kept solvent through government assistance (e.g., AIG). The interconnectedness of large financial intermediaries deemed "too-big-to-fail" heightened concerns about systemic risk, which can be understood as the failure of one firm leading to system-wide disruptions. One channel through which systemic risk can spread, as discussed in this report, is a disruption, such as the failure of a "too-big-to-fail" institution, cascading through PCS systems or activities.

AIG, a major insurance company, experienced a crisis stemming from a subsidiary that was a leading underwriter of credit default swaps (CDS), a type of over-the-counter derivative.[3] CDS provide protection to buyers against credit events such as an issuer's default on corporate debt obligations and structured securities. CDS had been traded bilaterally between institutions through an over-the-counter market system that regulatory authorities had criticized for its inefficiencies and lack of transparency. The Federal Reserve Bank of New York undertook efforts to encourage industry participants to voluntarily improve the infrastructure of the OTC derivatives market in recent years. In 2006, Alan Greenspan, then-Chairman of the Federal Reserve, reportedly said that he was appalled that people were relying on scraps of paper to record transactions, a practice which some blamed for causing a backlog of unconfirmed contracts.[4]

Prior to the Dodd-Frank Act, various federal regulatory authorities had oversight responsibilities for certain systems or entities engaged in processing those financial transactions. Title VIII reflects recommendations by the previous and current administrations to give the Federal Reserve explicit statutory oversight authority with respect to elements of the financial infrastructure in the United States, while also giving similar authority to the Securities and Exchange Commission (SEC) and Commodity Futures Trading Commission (CFTC) for certain parts of the

---

[1] P.L. 111-203, the *Dodd-Frank Wall Street Reform and Consumer Protection Act*.

[2] See Federal Reserve Fedwire Funds Services website at http://www.federalreserve.gov/paymentsystems/fedfunds_ann.htm, and CHIPS annual statistics at http://www.chips.org/about/pages/001221.php. 2011 figures from Fedwire and CHIPS were added together.

[3] U.S. Department of the Treasury, *Blueprint for a Modernized Financial Regulatory Structure*, Washington, DC, March 2008, p. 102. AIG was also exposed to significant losses from its securities lending operation.

[4] John Glover and Hamish Risk, "Exchange-Traded Credit Derivatives Poised to Curb Bank Monopoly," *Bloomberg*, December 11, 2006.

infrastructure. Title VIII introduces the term "financial market utility" (FMU or utility) for those multilateral systems that transfer, clear, or settle payments, securities, or other financial transactions among financial institutions (FI) or between a FMU and a financial institution. Title VIII addresses the federal regulatory oversight of systemically important payment, clearing, and settlement (PCS) systems and PCS activities of financial institutions that facilitate various financial transactions. Financial transactions processed daily in the U.S. economy include payment transfers ranging from small-dollar retail purchase transactions to large-value purchases of securities; clearing transactions for derivatives trading; and securities settlement.

Title VIII regulatory powers apply specifically to those financial market utilities and PCS activities (of financial institutions) that are designated as systemically important by the Financial Stability Oversight Council (FSOC), also created by the Dodd-Frank Act. It is notable that Title VIII does not consolidate or centralize authority for the approval of the formation of new utilities or PCS activities with the Federal Reserve or any single regulatory agency. Prior to the enactment of Title VIII, the Federal Reserve derived its oversight responsibilities for payment and settlement systems from a range of statutory responsibilities for monetary policy, banking supervision, lender of last resort, and provision of payment and settlement services.[5] Recently, the Federal Reserve released a final rule regarding FMUs.[6] On July 18, 2012, FSOC voted unanimously to designate eight FMUs as systemically important (see "FMUs Designated by the FSOC"). FSOC did not designate any PCS activities as systemically important at that time.

Title VIII primarily addresses the regulatory framework rather than affecting the flows of funds through existing payment and settlement systems. TitleVII addresses the derivatives clearing systems and activities for OTC swap transactions.[7]

Some Representatives opposed Title VIII and struck the title governing PCS supervision from the financial reform bill that the House of Representatives passed in December 2009. Concerns held by some opponents of the title may have included a sense that the U.S. financial infrastructure was adequately supervised, or that the title might have given too much discretionary authority to the Federal Reserve. Other reservations may have included the view that Title VIII was unnecessary in light of the Federal Reserve's efforts to encourage firms to voluntarily strengthen infrastructure procedures in various markets, and the absence of a PCS-related breakdown in September 2008. S. 3497, introduced on August 2, 2012, seeks to repeal Title VIII, stripping FSOC of its authority to designate FMUs as systemically important.

This report begins by introducing the major PCS systems operating in the United States, followed by the basics of PCS systems and activities. The report then describes the different risks, including systemic risk, that are commonly associated with PCS systems and activities. The next part of the report discusses the oversight authority of the FMU and FI regulators that was in place prior to the enactment of the Dodd-Frank Act, after which the report summarizes the changes made by Title VIII, including the new regulatory oversight authority of the Fed. The final part of

---

[5] Bank for International Settlements, Committee on Payment and Settlement Systems, *Central Bank Oversight of Payment and Settlement Systems*, CPSS Publications No. 68, Basel, Switzerland, May 2005, p. 13, http://www.bis.org/publ/cpss68.pdf. Hereinafter cited as BIS, *Central Bank Oversight*.

[6] Board of Governors of the Federal Reserve System, *Financial Market Utilties*, RIN No. 7100-AD 71, July 30, 2012, http://www.federalreserve.gov/newsevents/press/bcreg/bcreg20120730a1.pdf.

[7] See CRS Report R41398, *The Dodd-Frank Wall Street Reform and Consumer Protection Act: Title VII, Derivatives*, by Mark Jickling and Kathleen Ann Ruane.

the report addresses implementation of Title VIII by relevant agencies and the impact of Title VIII on FMUs and FIs.

Major Payment, Clearing, and Settlement Systems in the United States

The Federal Reserve and the private sector operate the systems that constitute the infrastructure for the processing and completion of financial transactions in the United States. Listed below are some of the major systems currently operating in the United States. Some privately-operated systems have been designated by FSOC as systemically important under Title VIII. Additional information regarding selected systems, including recent transaction volume levels, is set forth in an **Appendix** to this report. In the future, new and evolving types of financial products, transactions and instruments could lead to new payment, clearing, and settlement systems and activities.

FMUs Designated by the FSOC

On July 18, 2012, FSOC voted unanimously to designate eight FMUs as systemically important. Each was assigned a supervisory agency on the basis of the types of activities that they perform. The eight systemically important FMUs are:

- The Clearing House Payments Company, on the basis of its role as operator of the Clearing House Interbank Payments System (CHIPS).[8]
  (Supervisory Agency—The Federal Reserve)

- CLS Bank (foreign exchange)
  (Supervisory Agency—The Federal Reserve)

- Chicago Mercantile Exchange (CME) Clearing (credit default and interest rate swaps)
  (Supervisory Agency—Commodity Futures Trading Commission)

- Depository Trust Company (DTC)
  (Supervisory Agency—Securities and Exchange Commission)

- Fixed Income Clearing Corporation operating the Government Securities Division (GSD) and the Mortgage-Backed Securities Division (MBSD)
  (Supervisory Agency—Securities and Exchange Commission)

- ICE Trust (credit default swaps)
  (Supervisory Agency—Commodity Futures Trading Commission)

- National Securities Clearing Corporation (NSCC)
  (Supervisory Agency—Securities and Exchange Commission

---

[8] The Electronic Payments Network and other subsidiaries are deemed systemically important by default for being component parts of the parent company The Clearing House Payments Company, which was designated systemically important.

- The Options Clearing Corporation (equity derivatives)
  (Supervisory Agency—Securities and Exchange Commission)

The Clearing House operates an interbank funds transfer system known as CHIPS and an ACH system known as EPN. DTCC operates the Depository Trust Company (DTC), the major U.S. depository, and clearing corporations for government, mortgage-backed, and corporate and municipal securities. These entities provide the primary infrastructure for the clearance, settlement, and custody of the vast majority of transactions in the United States involving equities, corporate debt, municipal bonds, money market instruments, and government securities.[9] In the future, FSOC may add or remove PCS systems from the designated list, as conditions warrant.

Systems Operated by the Federal Reserve

The Federal Reserve Banks operate the following three wholesale payment services and an electronic payment system providing ACH services to depository institutions:

- Fedwire® Funds Service
- Fedwire Securities Service, also known as the National Book-Entry System (NBES)
- National Settlement Service (NSS)
- FedACH® Service

The Federal Reserve Banks began providing services using telecommunications in the early 1900s to transfer funds between accounts maintained in different Federal Reserve Districts.[10] In 1981, the Federal Reserve was required by law to price most of the Federal Reserve Bank financial services, including funds transfers and securities safekeeping, and to give nonmember depository institutions direct access to those services.[11] The Fedwire services enable depository institutions, the U.S. Treasury and other government agencies to transfer funds and book-entry securities nationwide. The Fedwire Funds Services is a real-time gross settlement (RTGS) system to settle funds electronically between banks; the Fedwire Securities Service provides issuance, settlement, and transfer services for U.S. Treasury securities and other government-related securities; and the National Settlement Service, which is a multilateral settlement service, is used by clearinghouses, financial exchanges, and other clearing and settlement groups. The Fedwire funds and securities transactions are processed in real time when received and are final and irrevocable when settled. By increasing the efficiency of Federal Reserve open market operations and helping to keep the market for government securities liquid, the Fedwire Securities Service plays a significant role in how the Federal Reserve conducts monetary policy,[12] which is commonly understood as the regulation of the money supply and interest rates by central banks.

---

[9] U.S. Department of the Treasury, *Blueprint for a Modernized Financial Regulatory Structure*, Washington, DC, March 2008, p. 211.

[10] Federal Reserve Bank of New York, *Fedwire and National Settlement Services*, New York, New York. http://www.newyorkfed.org/aboutthefed/fedpoint/fed43.html.

[11] The relevant law is the Depository Institutions Deregulation and Monetary Control Act of 1980, P.L. 96-221, enacted on March 31, 1980.

[12] Federal Reserve Bank of New York, *Fedwire and National Settlement Services*, New York, New York, http://www.newyorkfed.org/aboutthefed/fedpoint/fed43.html.

Open market operations, which are purchases and sales of U.S. Treasury and federal agency securities, are the Federal Reserve's principal tool for implementing monetary policy.[13]

When the FSOC designated the private sector FMUs in July 2012, the Fed "reaffirmed its long-standing policy of applying relevant international risk-management standards to the Federal Reserve Banks' Fedwire funds and Fedwire securities services."[14]

Other Systems Operated by the Private Sector

There are other smaller or foreign-based PCS systems that FSOC did not designate as FMUs in 2012. For example, the Depository Trust & Clearing Corporation (DTCC) also operates other essential, though not systemically important, private-sector systems in the United States. These systems are a group of DTCC subsidiaries, which include Euro CCP, AVOX and FICC among others. Some foreign-based systems provided PCS services for U.S. financial actors. For example, the Society for Worldwide Interbank Financial Telecommunication (SWIFT) is an international financial messaging system headquartered in Belgium with U.S. operations, and LCH.Clearnet is an important clearinghouse for several categories of assets.

The **Appendix** to this report provides additional information regarding these systems.

Basics of Payment, Clearing, and Settlement

The existing infrastructure in the United States for those activities consists of systems operated by the Federal Reserve through the Federal Reserve Banks, and by the private sector. In some cases, PCS activities are conducted primarily through one central party, such as the Fed or a clearinghouse. In other cases, activities are also conducted bilaterally through two financial institutions. This section describes the definitions and functions of these systems and activities that may partly overlap.

The following types of systems and activities are covered by Title VIII:

- payment systems, which transfer funds electronically from one institution to another;
- clearing systems (or clearinghouses), which in the derivatives market often transfer credit risk to a central counterparty (CCP) (clearinghouse) from each counterparty to a trade; and
- settlement systems, which complete transactions such as securities trades.

---

[13] Board of Governors of the Federal Reserve System, *Open Market Operations*, Washington, DC, January 26, 2010, http://www.federalreserve.gov/monetarypolicy/openmarket.htm.

[14] Federal Reserve, *Press Release*, July 19, 2012, available at http://www.federalreserve.gov/newsevents/press/bcreg/20120719a.htm.

Payment Systems

In general terms, a payment system consists of the means for transferring money between suppliers and users of funds through the use of cash substitutes such as checks, drafts, and electronic funds transfers. The Committee on Payment and Settlement Systems (CPSS), consisting of representatives from several international regulatory authorities, has developed generally accepted definitions of standard payment system terminology.[15] As defined by the CPSS, a *payment system* is a system that consists of a set of instruments, banking procedures, and, typically, interbank funds transfer systems that ensure the circulation of money.

In the United States, the Federal Reserve Banks and the private sector operate payment systems that process retail or wholesale transactions.[16] Retail payment systems facilitate a consumer's ability to purchase goods and services, pay bills, obtain cash through withdrawals and advances, and make person-to-person payments. Retail payments tend to generate a large number of transactions that have relatively small value per transaction and are processed through electronic funds transfer systems, including automated clearing house (ACH) transactions and debit and credit card transactions at the point of sale.[17]

The ACH is an electronic funds transfer (EFT) system that processes credit and debit transactions such as direct deposit payroll and consumer bill payments. ACH is the primary EFT system used by federal governmental agencies to make payments, according to the Financial Management Service (FMS), a bureau of the United States Department of the Treasury.[18] Providers of ACH services include the Federal Reserve Banks through the FedACH Service and The Electronic Payments Network, which is the only private-sector ACH operator in the United States.[19] Rules governing the ACH system for participating financial institutions are established by NACHA – The Electronic Payments Association, a trade association,[20] which oversees the ACH Network, and by the Federal Reserve.[21] NACHA reports that more than 20.2 billion ACH payments were made in 2011.[22]

Wholesale payment systems generally support domestic and international commercial activities and financial market related activities. Large-value, wholesale funds transfer systems are used for purchasing, selling, or financing securities transactions; disbursing or repaying loans; settling real

---

[15] Bank for International Settlements, Committee for Payment and Settlement Systems, *A Glossary of Terms Used in Payments and Settlement Systems*, Basel, Switzerland, March 2003, http://www.bis.org/publ/cpss00b.pdf. Hereinafter cited as BIS, *Glossary*.

[16] For background information on retail and wholesale payment systems, see Federal Financial Institutions Examination Council, *Retail Payment Systems*, IT Examination Handbook, Washington, DC, February 2010, http://www.ffiec.gov/ffiecinfobase/booklets/Retail/retail.pdf, hereinafter cited as FFIEC, *Retail Handbook*; and Federal Financial Institutions Examination Council, *Wholesale Payment Systems*, IT Examination Handbook, Washington, DC, July 2004, http://www.ffiec.gov/ffiecinfobase/booklets/Wholesale/whole.pdf, hereinafter cited as FFIEC, *Wholesale Handbook*.

[17] FFIEC, *Retail Handbook*, p. 4. Retail payment instruments include check-based payments, card-based and other electronic payments such as electronic cash and electronic benefits transfer, and ACH transactions.

[18] See Financial Management Service website, http://www.fms.treas.gov/ach/index.html.

[19] See Electronic Payments Network website, http://www.epaynetwork.com/cms/services/001456.php.

[20] The trade association was formerly known as the National Automated Clearing House Association.

[21] ACH transfers between financial institutions are not considered check transactions, and thus are not subject to laws governing check processing. FFIEC, *Retail Handbook*, p. 10.

[22] NACHA—The Electronic Payments Association, *ACH Network Statistics*, Herndon, VA, 2010, http://www.nacha.org/c/ACHntwkstats.cfm, visited August 31, 2012.

estate transactions; and making large-value, time-critical payments (e.g., settling interbank purchases, Federal funds sales, or foreign exchange transactions).[23] Wholesale payments tend to have a large per-transaction value and a relatively small number of transactions generated daily and are processed through payment systems such as the Fedwire Funds Service (Fedwire)[24] and The Clearing House Interbank Payments System (CHIPS).[25] Wholesale payment systems also provide final clearing and settlement for a variety of retail payment systems at the end of the business day. Financial institutions use intra-bank systems to initiate, process, and transmit large-value payment orders internally and to interface with Fedwire and CHIPS.

Clearing Systems

Clearing systems conduct various activities related to payment, currency, securities or derivatives transactions. The CPSS defines a *clearing system* as a set of procedures whereby financial institutions present and exchange data or documents relating to funds or securities transfers to other financial institutions at a single location (clearing house). The procedures often include a mechanism to facilitate the establishment of net positions of participant obligations for settlement, a process known as netting.[26] A *clearing house* is a central location or central processing mechanism through which financial institutions agree to exchange payment instructions or other financial obligations such as securities. The term *clearing*, which is the process of transmitting, reconciling and possibly confirming payment orders or security transfer instructions prior to settlement, sometimes is used imprecisely to include settlement.

Two of the major types of clearing houses in the United States process securities and derivatives transactions. For securities transactions, a clearing corporation or a depository must register with the Securities and Exchange Commission (SEC) as a clearing agency (CA).[27] Clearing corporations clear member transactions, enable automated settlement of those trades, and often act as intermediaries in making settlements. They also guarantee the completion of all transactions and interpose themselves as parties to both sides of a transaction.[28]

Depositories maintain ownership records of securities on the books of the depository, hold securities certificates (physical securities are held in vaults), and make securities deliveries for settlements requiring delivery. Currently, the Depository Trust Company (DTC) is the primary U.S. securities depository.[29] The DTC is a subsidiary of The Depository & Clearing Corporation

---

[23] FFIEC, *Wholesale Handbook*, p. 3.

[24] Fedwire participants maintain a reserve or securities account with a Federal Reserve Bank. Direct access to Federal Reserve payment services is generally limited to deposit-taking institutions; however, non-depository institutions may indirectly use those services as customers of Federal Reserve payment services participants. Ibid, p.4.

[25] CHIPS is operated by The Clearing House, which also operates the Electronic Payments Network, a private-sector provider of ACH services. CHIPS' website is http://www.chips.org/home.php.

[26] The Committee on Payment and Settlement Services defines netting as an agreed offsetting of positions or obligations by trading partners or participants. Netting reduces a large number of individual positions or obligations to a smaller number and may take several forms that have varying degrees of legal enforceability in the event of default of one of the parties. BIS, *Glossary*.

[27] U.S. Securities and Exchange Commission, *Clearing Agencies*, Washington, DC, http://www.sec.gov/divisions/marketreg/mrclearing.shtml.

[28] Ibid.

[29] Ibid.

(DTCC),[30] which also operates the Fixed Income Clearing Corporation (FICC). FICC clears government and mortgage-backed securities through its clearing corporation divisions known as the Government Securities Division (GSD) and the Mortgage-Backed Securities Division (MBSD). In addition, the National Securities Clearing Corporation (NSCC), which is a subsidiary of DTCC, is a registered clearing corporation regulated by the SEC that provides clearing and settlement services for corporate and municipal securities.

In the futures and options markets, a clearing house, known as a derivatives clearing organization (DCO), must register with the Commodity Futures Trading Commission (CFTC) to provide clearing services with respect to futures contracts and options on those futures contracts traded on a designated contract market and swap transactions traded over-the-counter.[31] A DCO enables the parties to a derivatives transaction (counterparties) to transfer credit risk to the clearing house, for example, through novation. Novation occurs when a single derivatives contract between two counterparties becomes two separate contracts: one between the clearing house and each counterparty. As of August 2012, there were 25 DCOs registered with the CFTC.[32]

Settlement Systems

The CPSS defines *settlement*, in part, as the completion of a transaction wherein the seller transfers securities or financial instruments to the buyer and the buyer transfers money to the seller. A settlement may be final or provisional. A *settlement system* is used to facilitate the settlement of transfers of funds or financial instruments. In a *real-time gross settlement system* (RTGS), processing and settling occur on an order-by-order basis in real time instead of through netting of transaction positions. A *securities settlement system* is a particular kind of settlement system that consists of the full set of institutional arrangements for confirmation, clearance and settlement of securities trades and safekeeping of securities.

In the United States, the Federal Reserve Banks and the private sector operate different settlement systems for securities transactions. Securities processing within financial institutions and the major markets accounts for the majority of large-value payments.[33]

The major securities markets in the United States include the markets for government securities, corporate equities and bonds, money market instruments, and municipal bonds. Those instruments are generally traded through organized exchanges or through over-the-counter dealer markets.[34] Depository institutions play several important roles in securities clearing and settlement. In addition to participating in clearing and settlement transactions, depository institutions act as custodians, issuing and paying agents, and settling banks for their customers.

---

[30] The Depository Trust & Clearing Corporation, *About DTCC, Our Structure*, New York, New York, http://www.dtcc.com/about/subs/.

[31] U.S. Commodity Futures Trading Commission, *Clearing Organizations, Derivatives Clearing Organizations*, Washington, DC, http://www.cftc.gov/IndustryOversight/ClearingOrganizations/index.htm.

[32] http://sirt.cftc.gov/SIRT/SIRT.aspx?Topic=ClearingOrganizations&implicit=true&type=DCO&CustomColumnDisplay=TTTTTTTT.

[33] Federal Financial Institutions Examination Council, *Wholesale Payment Systems*, IT Examination Handbook Presentations, Washington, DC, July 2004, p. 3, http://www.ffiec.gov/ffiecinfobase/presentations/whole_presntation.pdf.

[34] FFIEC, *Wholesale Handbook*, p. 11.

The U.S. government securities market includes all primary and secondary market transactions in securities issued by the U.S. Treasury, certain federal government agencies, and federal government-sponsored enterprises.[35] Trading in government securities is conducted over-the-counter between brokers, dealers, and investors, which means that parties trade on a bilateral basis with one another rather than on an organized exchange. The Federal Reserve operates a book-entry system known as the National Book-Entry System, or the Fedwire Securities Service, through which nearly all U.S. government securities are issued and transferred.[36] The Fixed Income Clearing Corporation (FICC) also supports the selling and trading of U.S. government securities.

Corporations and municipal governments also issue various types of securities, including corporate equities and bonds, commercial paper,[37] and municipal bonds. Various securities are traded on established U.S. exchanges, including the New York Stock Exchange, the American Stock Exchange, and the NASDAQ system, and on over-the-counter markets. The National Securities Clearing Corporation (NSCC) provides clearing, settlement, and other services for virtually all broker-to-broker trades involving equities, corporate and municipal debt, and certain other instruments traded on over-the-counter markets and exchanges.[38]

Risks of Payment, Clearing, and Settlement Systems and Activities

Section 802 of the Dodd-Frank Act reflects concern about risks related to PCS systems and activities. For example, the proper functioning of the financial markets is considered dependent upon safe and efficient arrangements for the clearing and settlement of payment, securities, and other financial transactions. Although financial market utilities that conduct or support multilateral PCS activities may reduce risks for their participants and the broader financial system, such utilities may also concentrate and create new risks. Congress also found that PCS activities conducted by financial institutions present risks to the participating financial institutions and to the financial system. Congress found it necessary to enhance the regulation and supervision of utilities and PCS activities that are systemically important, in part, to reduce systemic risk and to promote safety and soundness.

Further, both the Bush and Obama Administrations addressed the risks arising from payment and settlement systems in proposing financial regulatory reforms. In those proposals for heightened supervision by the Federal Reserve, the U.S. Department of the Treasury noted concerns about

---

[35] Ibid.

[36] Ibid. The Federal Reserve Banks in their capacity as fiscal agents facilitate the issuance of book-entry securities to the Fedwire Securities Service participants. The Fedwire Securities system maintains in electronic form all marketable U.S. Treasury securities as well as many federal government agency, GSE, and certain international organizations' securities. See Federal Reserve Bank Services, *Fedwire Securities Service*, http://www.frbservices.org/serviceofferings/fedwire/fedwire_security_service.html.

[37] Commercial paper is a money market instrument issued by prime-rated non-financial and financial companies with maturities ranging from one to 270 days. Commercial paper is issued through dealer placements or direct placements with investors. Commercial paper is an important source of short-term funding for financial corporations and municipal governments and secondary market trading is limited. FFIEC, *Wholesale Handbook*, p. 14.

[38] The Depository Trust & Clearing Corporation, *About DTCC, National Securities Clearing Corporation (NSCC)*, New York, New York, http://www.dtcc.com/about/subs/nscc.php.

the ability of payment and settlement systems to contribute to financial crises, rather than reduce them, potentially threatening the stability of U.S. and foreign financial markets.[39]

Systemic Risk

There is no single definition of systemic risk. The Federal Reserve Bank of Cleveland has indicated that a firm is considered systemically important if its failure would have economically significant spillover effects which, if left unchecked, could destabilize the financial system and have a negative impact on the real economy.[40] In order to provide more guidance in practice, however, the Cleveland Fed proposes using the following four factors, other than size, for designating firms as systemically important: contagion, correlation, concentration, and conditions (context). The International Monetary Fund summarizes systemic risk as the large losses to other financial institutions induced by the failure of a particular interconnected institution.[41] Congress has addressed systemic risk in a number of provisions of the Dodd-Frank Act, in part, through the establishment of the Financial Stability Oversight Council and the regulation of systemically significant firms.[42]

Systemic risk can be increased by the transmission of financial system disruptions through payment and settlement systems. The global payment and settlement infrastructure consists of a network of domestic and cross-border systems that are increasingly connected through a wide array of complex interrelationships.[43] Financial market utilities, financial institutions, and other system participants are increasingly connected as operators of and participants in such systems.

Payment and settlement risks have the potential to impose losses on the entity at the source of a disruption as well as on its direct counterparties or customers, and in some circumstances, their counterparties or customers.[44] Financial institutions engage in a range of financial activities that require the settlement of obligations and transfer of assets, which can lead to principal credit losses or replacement costs when these transfers do not occur as expected.[45] The entity that is the source of an initial credit, liquidity or operational disruption, such as a failed securities trade or operational outage, may face lost revenue. That entity's customers and counterparties may face replacement costs from the purchase of additional funds or securities at a potentially higher market price to complete their own obligations. A settlement institution may also redistribute payment and settlement risks back to its participants through loss-sharing arrangements that may

---

[39] U.S. Department of the Treasury, *Blueprint for a Modernized Financial Regulatory Structure*, Washington, DC, March 2008, p. 101; U.S. Department of the Treasury, *Financial Regulatory Reform, A New Foundation: Rebuilding Financial Supervision and Regulation*, Washington, DC, June 2009, p. 52, http://www.financialstability.gov/docs/regs/FinalReport_web.pdf. Hereinafter cited as *2009 New Foundation*.

[40] James B. Thomson, *On Systemically Important Financial Institutions and Progressive Systemic Mitigation*, Federal Reserve Bank of Cleveland, Policy Discussion Paper Number 27, August 2009, p. 1, http://www.clevelandfed.org/research/policydis/pdp27.pdf.

[41] International Monetary Fund, *Meeting New Challenges to Stability and Building a Safer System*, Global Financial Stability Report, April 2010, p. 2, http://www.imf.org/external/pubs/ft/gfsr/2010/01/index.htm.

[42] For a discussion of provisions addressing systemic risk, see CRS Report R41384, *The Dodd-Frank Wall Street Reform and Consumer Protection Act: Systemic Risk and the Federal Reserve*, by Marc Labonte.

[43] Bank for International Settlements, Committee on Payment and Settlement Systems, *The Interdependencies of Payment and Settlement Systems*, CPSS Publications No. 84, Basel, Switzerland, June 2008, p. iii, http://www.bis.org/publ/cpss84.pdf.

[44] Ibid., p. 27.

[45] Ibid.

apply to participants that had no transactions with the failing entity. Further, some types of interdependencies among systems can allow an initial disruption to activate a chain of different risks and transmit an initial disruption through multiple systems.

The interdependencies of financial intermediaries thus increase the potential for disruptions to spread quickly and widely, including across multiple systems. Several factors over the past few decades have contributed to the development of such interdependencies.[46] These factors include the globalization and regional integration of the financial sector, consolidation of financial institutions, and advances in computer and telecommunications technology.

Events during the financial crisis of 2008 included the transmission of disruptions arising from the failure of large, interconnected financial institutions through payment, clearing, and settlement systems. In the view of some international banking regulators, the financial market infrastructures generally performed well during the recent financial crisis and did much to help prevent the crisis from becoming even more serious.[47] Those regulators have argued that when robust financial market infrastructures can enable settlement to take place without significant counterparty risk, such systems help markets to remain liquid even during times of financial stress.[48]

Some observers argue that another source of systemic risk could be the clearing house that functions as a central counterparty, i.e., the buyer to every seller and the seller to every buyer, in derivatives transactions.[49] That risk arguably could increase because of the Title VII provisions requiring the clearing of swaps transactions under certain circumstances. In addition, academics are studying whether the use of central clearing counterparties actually reduces counterparty risk.[50] In Title VIII, Congress indicated that financial market utilities may also concentrate and create new risks and stated that such utilities must be well designed and operated in a safe and sound manner.[51]

Other Risks

In addition to systemic risk, the Federal Reserve has identified the following four basic risks in payment and settlement systems:

- **credit risk**, which is the risk that a counterparty will not settle an obligation for full value either when due, or anytime thereafter;

- **liquidity risk**, which is the risk that a counterparty will not settle an obligation for full value when due;

---

[46] Ibid., p. 14.

[47] Bank for International Settlements, "Standards for Payment, Clearing, and Settlement Systems: Review by CPSS-IOSCO," Basel, Switzerland, press release, February 2, 2010, http://www.bis.org/press/p100202.htm. Hereinafter cited as BIS, *Standards Review Press Release*.

[48] Ibid.

[49] See, e.g., Elena Logutenkova and Fabio Benedetti-Valentini, "Blankfein Says Clearinghouses May Increase Risks in Crisis," *Bloomberg Businessweek*, September 29, 2010, http://www.businessweek.com/news/2010-09-29/blankfein-says-clearinghouses-may-increase-risks-in-crisis.html.

[50] Darrell Duffie and Haoxiang Zhu, "Does a Central Clearing Counterparty Reduce Counterparty Risk?," *Graduate School of Business, Stanford University*, Updated March 6, 2010, p. http://www.stanford.edu/~duffie/DuffieZhu.pdf.

[51] Section 802(a)(2) of the Dodd-Frank Act, P.L. 111-203.

- **operational risk**, which is the risk of loss resulting from inadequate or failed internal processes, people, and systems, or from external events, and which includes various physical and information security risks; and

- **legal risk**, which is the risk of loss because of the unexpected application of a law or regulation or because a contract cannot be enforced.[52]

These risks can, but need not, lead to systemic risk. Due to the potential for significant loss resulting from the large dollar value of wholesale payments, regulators expect financial institutions to implement effective and appropriate risk management policies, procedures, and controls to protect against such risks as well as reputation and strategic risk.[53] Institutions involved with wholesale payments must also manage legal and compliance risk under laws administered by the Office of Foreign Assets Control imposing economic sanctions against specified foreign countries and individuals and by the record-keeping and reporting requirements of the Bank Secrecy Act, as amended by the USA PATRIOT Act.[54]

Operational risks arising from wholesale payments include risks relating to internal and operational controls, audit, information security, business continuity planning, and vendor and third-party management. Security risk may arise from intra-bank funds transfers. A financial institution's funds transfer operation, often known as "the wire room," is responsible for originating, transmitting, and receiving payment orders. Financial institutions must establish the authenticity of incoming and outgoing funds transfer messages and the time of receipt of incoming payment orders.[55]

Regulatory Oversight Prior to Title VIII

Recommendations to Strengthen Oversight

Prior to Title VIII, an entity's supervisory agency, and for certain entities, the Federal Reserve, conducted prudential oversight of payment, clearing, and settlement systems and activities of financial institutions.[56] The Federal Reserve relied on "a patchwork of authorities, largely derived from [its] role as a banking supervisor, as well as on moral suasion" as a means to help ensure that payment and settlement systems had necessary procedures and controls in place to manage their risks.[57] In 2008, the Chairman of the Federal Reserve System asked Congress for authority to oversee systemically important payment and settlement systems, noting that many major central banks around the world have that explicit statutory authority.[58] In that testimony, Chairman Bernanke stated that "the stability of the broader financial system requires key payment

---

[52] Board of Governors of the Federal Reserve System, *Policy on Payment System Risk*, Washington, DC, as amended effective June 16, 2010, http://federalreserve.gov/paymentsystems/psr_policy.htm.

[53] See FFIEC, *Wholesale Handbook*, p. 21.

[54] Ibid., p. 27.

[55] Ibid., p. 18.

[56] See the discussion of prudential regulators in the next section of this report.

[57] *Statement of Ben S. Bernanke, Chairman, Board of Governors of the Federal Reserve System*, in U.S. Congress, House Committee on Financial Services, *Systemic Risk and the Financial Markets*, 110th Cong., 2nd sess., July 10, 2008, H.Hrg., p. 65 (Washington: GPO, 2008).

[58] Ibid.

and settlement systems to operate smoothly under stress and to effectively manage counterparty risk."[59]

Prior to the enactment of Title VIII, United States and international regulatory authorities called for the strengthening of the supervisory oversight of the financial infrastructure for payment and settlement systems. The U.S. Department of the Treasury issued reports during both the Bush and Obama Administrations recommending that oversight of systemically important payment and settlement systems should be given to the Federal Reserve.[60]

The Federal Reserve, together with other regulators and the private sector, was also engaged in efforts to strengthen various financial infrastructures prior to the Dodd-Frank Act. In 2005, the Federal Reserve Bank of New York began leading an initiative with industry participants to strengthen clearing and settling of credit default swaps and other OTC derivatives.[61] In addition, the Federal Reserve Bank of New York has worked with the private sector to enhance the oversight of tri-party repurchase agreements (repos[62]).[63]

Pre-Dodd-Frank Oversight

Prior to the Dodd-Frank Act, the Federal Reserve had prudential oversight responsibilities for key private-sector infrastructure systems, including CHIPS, CLS, DTCC (and its three primary subsidiaries, DTC, NSCC, and FICC), ICE Trust, and SWIFT.[64] The Federal Reserve had authority to oversee certain firms or their PCS activities under its statutory authority to conduct monetary policy and banking supervision, to act as the lender of last resort, and to supervise the Federal Reserve Banks' provision of payment and settlement services.[65] Other federal and state regulatory agencies also exercised prudential oversight of PCS systems and activities within their supervisory jurisdiction. For example, DTC was supervised by the New York State Banking Department based on its charter as a limited-purpose trust company under New York law. In addition, DTC was regulated by the Federal Reserve as a Fed member institution and by the SEC as a registered clearing agency.

---

[59] Ibid.

[60] U.S. Department of the Treasury, *Blueprint for a Modernized Financial Regulatory Structure*, Washington, DC, March 2008; *2009 New Foundation*.

[61] Federal Reserve Bank of New York, "Statement Regarding Meeting on Credit Derivatives," press release, New York, New York, September 15, 2005, http://www.newyorkfed.org/newsevents/news_archive/markets/2005/an050915.html. For information on developments from this initiative, see Federal Reserve Bank of New York, *OTC Derivatives Market Infrastructure*, New York, New York, http://www.newyorkfed.org/newsevents/otc_derivative.html.

[62] A repo transaction is an agreement between two parties on the sale and subsequent repurchase of securities at an agreed price. In economic terms, a repo transaction is equivalent to a loan backed by collateral consisting of the securities. Bank for International Settlements, Committee on Payment and Settlement Systems, *Strengthening Repo Clearing and Settlement Arrangements*, CPSS Publications No. 91, Basel, Switzerland, September 2010, p. 5, http://www.bis.org/publ/cpss91.pdf. Hereinafter cited as BIS, *Strengthening Repo*.

[63] The Payments Risk Committee is a private sector group representing various U.S. banks. The Payments Risk Committee is sponsored by the Federal Reserve Bank of New York. See Federal Reserve Bank of New York, *Payments Risk Committee*, New York, New York, http://www.newyorkfed.org/prc/. In May 2010, the Federal Reserve Bank of New York released a white paper on Tri-Party Repurchase Agreement (Repo) Reform. Federal Reserve Bank of New York, *Tri-Party Repo Infrastructure Reform*, White Paper, New York, New York, May 17, 2010, http://www.newyorkfed.org/banking/nyfrb_triparty_whitepaper.pdf.

[64] See Board of Governors of the Federal Reserve System, *Oversight of Key Financial Market Infrastructures, Private-Sector Systems*, Washington, DC, http://www.federalreserve.gov/paymentsystems/over_pssystems.htm.

[65] BIS, *Central Bank Oversight*, p. 13.

The Federal Reserve also has supervisory authority (under the Federal Reserve Act) with respect to the Federal Reserve Banks' operation of key payment and settlement systems, including the Fedwire Funds Service and the Fedwire Securities Service. The Federal Reserve Board sets policy and is responsible for general supervision and oversight of the Federal Reserve Banks, including the provision of payment services.[66] Under such authority, the Federal Reserve conducts regular reviews of these systems and periodic assessments of the Fedwire Services against the relevant international standards.

The prudential regulators include the CFTC for derivatives clearing organizations, the SEC for clearing agencies, and the federal bank regulatory agencies for depository institutions. Prior to the enactment of the Dodd-Frank Act, the SEC regulated clearing agencies (CAs) under the authority of the Exchange Act, sections 17, 17A and 19. CAs had to register with the SEC but were considered self-regulating organizations (SROs). Registration required compliance with established rules and a list of organizational and capacity standards. Because CAs are SROs though, little more was required of them other than filing to register with the SEC. Although they had to provide SEC any proposed changes to their rules, and self-enforce compliance to ensure that participants abided by these rules, CAs established the rules for their own industry.[67] While the SEC has maintained the authority to adopt rules for CAs deemed necessary and appropriate to the public interest, Dodd-Frank looks to codify more specifically enhanced risk management standards.

The CFTC, for its part, had regulatory authority over derivatives clearing organizations (DCO) under the Commodities Exchange Act (CEA). A DCO had to register with the CFTC and comply with 18 core principles in order to maintain its registration. The core principles ranged in topic from risk management to default rules to information sharing, among others. DCOs were granted authority to implement their own rules, but they had to comply with the CEA and be approved by the CFTC. While the CFTC program takes a "risk-based approach," Title VII and VIII state more explicitly how DCOs are to operate.[68]

Supervisory Policies

The Federal Reserve Policy on Payment System Risk (PSR Policy) addresses the risks that payment and settlement activity present to the financial system and the Federal Reserve Banks.[69] The PSR Policy sets out the Board's views, principles and minimum standards applicable to risk management for private-sector and Federal Reserve Bank payment and settlement systems.[70] In

---

[66] Board of Governors of the Federal Reserve System, *Oversight of Key Financial Market Infrastructures, Reserve Bank Systems*, Washington, DC, http://www.federalreserve.gov/paymentsystems/over_rbsystems.htm.

[67] Board of Governors of the Federal Reserve, Securities and Exchange Commission, and Commodity Futures Trading Commission, *Risk Management Supervision of Designated Clearing Entities*, Securities and Exchange Commission, Washington, DC, July 1, 2011, pp. 19-22, http://www.sec.gov/news/studies/2011/813study.pdf.

[68] Board of Governors of the Federal Reserve, Securities and Exchange Commission, and Commodity Futurees Trading Commission, *Risk Management Supervision of Desginated Clearing Entities*, Securities and Exchange Commission, Washington, DC, July 2011, pp. 22-24, http://www.sec.gov/news/studies/2011/813study.pdf.

[69] The current PSR Policy, as amended effective June 16, 2010, is effective through March 23, 2011 and is accessible at http://www.federalreserve.gov/paymentsystems/psr_policy.htm. The PSR Policy that will become effective on March 24, 2011 is accessible at http://www.federalreserve.gov/paymentsystems/2011_psr_policy.htm.

[70] The PSR Policy also governs the provision of intraday or "daylight" credit provided by Federal Reserve Banks, including policies regarding overdrafts in accounts at Federal Reserve Banks, net debit caps, and daylight overdraft fees.

addition, the Federal Reserve's Regulation F requires insured depository institutions to establish policies and procedures to avoid excessive exposures to any other depository institutions, including those created through the clearing and settlement of payments.[71]

Bank supervision guidelines include the 2003 *Interagency Paper on Sound Practices to Strengthen the Resilience of the U.S. Financial System* adopted by the Federal Reserve, SEC and OCC to improve the resilience of the private-sector clearing and settlement infrastructure following the events of September 11, 2001.[72] The goal of the Interagency Paper was to ensure the smooth operation of the financial system in the event of a wide-scale disruption.

A 2008 interagency agreement among the Federal Reserve, the CFTC, and the SEC reflects the agencies' intent to cooperate and share information in carrying out their respective regulatory and supervisory responsibilities with regard to central counterparties for credit default swaps.[73]

The CFTC has also entered into an international interagency agreement with the United Kingdom Financial Services Authority (FSA) regarding derivatives clearing organizations and clearing houses based in the UK. In 2009, the CFTC and FSA signed a memorandum of understanding (MOU) that establishes a framework expressing their willingness to cooperate in the interest of fulfilling their statutory functions with respect to the clearing organizations, including on-site visits of respective clearing organizations.[74]

International Regulatory Standards

International banking regulators have also taken actions to identify risks related to PCS systems and to strengthen the financial infrastructure. The Committee for Payments and Settlement Systems (CPSS) was set up in 1990 under the aegis of the Bank for International Settlements (BIS) by the central banks of the Group of 10[75] countries. In 2009, the CPSS enlarged its membership to include many other important central banks. The CPSS meets three times annually and promotes sound and efficient payment and settlement systems. The CPSS acts as an international standard-setting body for payment and securities settlement systems and as a forum for central banks to monitor and analyze developments in domestic PCS systems and cross-border and multicurrency settlement systems.[76]

---

[71] 12 C.F.R. Part 206.

[72] Dated April 7, 2003. Issued with Board of Governors of the Federal Reserve System, *Federal Reserve Supervisory Letter SR 03-9*, Washington, DC, May 28, 2003, http://www.federalreserve.gov/boarddocs/srletters/2003/sr0309.htm.

[73] U.S. Department of the Treasury, "Memorandum of Understanding Between the Board, the CFTC, and the SEC Regarding Central Counterparties for Credit Default Swaps," press release, Washington, DC, November 14, 2008, http://www.ustreas.gov/press/releases/hp1272.htm.

[74] U.S. Commodity Futures Trading Commission, Memorandum of Understanding Concerning Cooperation and the Exchange of Information Related to the Supervision of Cross-Border Clearing Organizations, Washington, DC, September 14, 2009, http://www.cftc.gov/ucm/groups/public/@internationalaffairs/documents/file/ukfsa09.pdf.

[75] The Group of 10 or G10 includes the United States, the United Kingdom, Germany, France, Canada, Japan, Sweden, Italy, Switzerland, the Netherlands and Belgium (11 countries).

[76] Bank for International Settlements, *Committee on Payment and Settlement Systems, CPSS Publications*, Basel, Switzerland, http://www.bis.org/cpss/index.htm. The current chairman of the CPSS is William C. Dudley, President of the Federal Reserve Bank of New York. Timothy Geithner, then-President and Chief Executive Officer of the Federal Reserve Bank of New York, chaired the CPSS from 2005 to 2009. See Bank for International Settlements, *CPSS History, Organisation, Cooperation*, Basel, Switzerland, http://www.bis.org/cpss/cpssinfo01.htm.

The standards consist of the Core Principles for Systemically Important Payment Systems (January 2001)[77] and two sets of recommendations published together with IOSCO (International Organization of Securities Commissions),[78] the Recommendations for Securities Settlement Systems (November 2001)[79] and the Recommendations for Central Counterparties (May 2004).[80] In February 2010, the CPSS and IOSCO launched a comprehensive review of the three sets of standards for financial market infrastructures with a view to strengthening them where appropriate.[81]

The CPSS also publishes policy reports analyzing issues related to large-value payment systems, retail payment instruments and systems, settlement mechanisms for foreign exchange transactions, and clearing and settlement of securities and derivatives transactions.[82] A CPSS report from May 2005 expressed the view that a core responsibility of central banks is the oversight function with respect to payment and settlement systems.[83]

In September 2010, the CPSS published a report entitled *Strengthening Repo Clearing and Settlement Arrangements* after the repo markets proved to be a less reliable source of funding liquidity than expected in some countries during the recent financial crisis.[84]

The CPSS published another report in April 2012 entitled *Principles for Financial Market Infrastructures, Assessment Methodology and Disclosure Framework*.[85] The report establishes international standards for payment, clearing and settlement systems, including central counterparties, that are more demanding than previous standards. The new set of standards replaces the previous set. The new standards raise minimum risk requirements, provide more specific guidance, and increase the number of institutions under its purview. Members of CPSS have been encouraged to adopt the new standards by the end of 2012.

Title VIII of the Dodd-Frank Act

Title VIII of the *Dodd-Frank Wall Street Reform and Consumer Protection Act*, P.L. 111-203 establishes a regulatory framework for systemically important utilities and systemically important

---

[77] Bank for International Settlements, Committee on Payment and Settlement Systems, CPSS Publications No. 43, Basel, Switzerland, http://www.bis.org/publ/cpss43.pdf.

[78] IOSCO is a policy forum for securities regulators whose membership regulates more than 95% of the world's securities markets in over 100 jurisdictions.

[79] Bank for International Settlements, Committee on Payment and Settlement Systems, CPSS Publications No. 46, Basel, Switzerland, http://www.bis.org/publ/cpss46.pdf.

[80] Bank for International Settlements, Committee on Payment and Settlement Systems, CPSS Publications No. 64, Basel, Switzerland, http://www.bis.org/publ/cpss64.pdf.

[81] BIS, *Standards Review Press Release*. The CPSS expects to issue draft revised standards by early 2011. The International Monetary Fund and the World Bank are also participating in the CPSS-IOSCO standards review, which is part of the Financial Stability Board's work to reduce the risks that arise from interconnectedness in the financial system.

[82] See Bank for International Settlements, *Committee on Payment and Settlement Systems, CPSS Publications*, http://www.bis.org/cpss/index.htm.

[83] BIS, *Central Bank Oversight*, p. iii.

[84] BIS, *Strengthening Repo*.

[85] Committee on Payment and Settlement Systems, *Principles for Financial Market Infrastructures*, Bank for International Settlements, Basel, Switzerland, April 1, 2012, http://www.bis.org/publ/cpss101a.pdf.

PCS activities conducted by financial institutions. It provides explicit statutory oversight authority to the Federal Reserve (Fed) in coordination with an entity's chartering and supervisory authority, establishing a consistent framework across supervisory authorities.

The Dodd-Frank Act also affects PCS systems and activities through Title VII, the *Wall Street Transparency and Accountability Act of 2010*, which establishes a comprehensive regulatory framework in regard to the over-the-counter (OTC) derivatives market and swap transactions.[86] Title VII establishes requirements for the clearing of certain bilateral swap transactions through derivatives clearinghouses. Title VII also strengthens regulatory oversight of designated clearing entities (registered derivatives clearing organizations and clearing agencies) by the CFTC and the SEC, which are subject to the regulatory framework established in Title VIII.

The Senate, but not the House of Representatives, passed a version of the financial reform bill containing a title similar to Title VIII.[87] The House Financial Services Committee considered but struck by amendment a similar title in mark up, prior to the House of Representatives' floor consideration of the financial reform bill, H.R. 4173. Both the version of Title VIII in the Senate's bill and the version offered in the Conference Committee were modeled on proposed legislation released by the Obama Administration in 2009.[88] During the Conference Committee, participants agreed to changes that enhanced the authority of the CFTC and SEC with respect to their supervised entities. The changes to the relevant title gave the CFTC and the SEC rule-writing authority for risk management standards and excluded some of their supervised entities from definitions and Federal Reserve oversight.

Title VIII defines *systemically important* and *systemic importance* apply to a situation where the failure of or a disruption to the functioning of a financial market utility or the conduct of a PCS activity could create or increase the risk of significant liquidity or credit problems spreading among financial institutions or markets and thereby threaten the stability of the financial system of the United States.

In general, Title VIII defines a *supervisory agency* as the federal agency that has primary jurisdiction over a designated financial market utility under federal banking, securities, or commodity futures laws and means the SEC with respect to a registered clearing agency, the CFTC with respect to a registered derivatives clearing organization, the appropriate federal banking agency with respect to an institution described in section 3(q) of the Federal Deposit Insurance Act, and the Federal Reserve Board with respect to any other type of designated financial market utility.

Exclusions

Title VIII broadly defines FMU systems and activities, but then explicitly excludes several specific systems and activities from its scope. Section 803 of Title VIII excludes from the FMU

---

[86] See CRS Report R41398, *The Dodd-Frank Wall Street Reform and Consumer Protection Act: Title VII, Derivatives*, by Mark Jickling and Kathleen Ann Ruane.

[87] S. 3217 contained the language of the Senate version of the financial reform bill. The Senate passed H.R. 4173, with an amendment in the nature of a substitute, replacing the House language with the text of S. 3217.

[88] U.S. Department of the Treasury, *Title VIII*, Washington, DC, http://www.financialstability.gov/docs/regulatoryreform/title-VIII_payments_072209.pdf. For information on all of the proposed titles, see U.S. Department of the Treasury, http://www.financialstability.gov/roadtostability/timeline.html.

definition specified registered trading entities (exchanges) and data repositories registered and subject to CFTC oversight, including designated contract markets and swap data repositories, or registered and subject to SEC oversight, including national securities exchanges and swap execution facilities. Those exclusions are limited to the activities that require the entities to be registered.

Other exclusions from the FMU definition apply to various parties that act as intermediaries, including any broker, dealer, transfer agent, investment company, futures commission merchant, introducing broker, commodity trading advisor, or commodity pool operator. Such exclusions are limited to functions performed as part of the institution's named business. Also excluded are activities conducted by such institutions on behalf of a FMU or an FMU participant so long as the activities are not part of the FMU's critical risk management or processing functions.

Section 803 excludes from the financial institutions (FI) definition *designated clearing entities*, which are the systemically important DCOs and CAs subject to oversight by the CFTC and the SEC, respectively. The exclusion applies to the activities that require the entity to be registered. Thus, Title VIII regulation could apply to those entities only as FMUs rather than FIs.

Section 803 also excludes from the FI definition those registered trading entities (exchanges) and data repositories subject to CFTC or SEC oversight that are excluded from the definition of an FMU, such as designated contract markets, swap data repositories, and swap execution facilities, and additionally other entities, including securities information processors. The exclusion applies to the activities that require the entity to be registered.

FSOC Determines Systemic Importance

Congress provides a role to the newly created Financial Stability Oversight Council (Council) in the enhanced regulatory oversight framework in Title VIII. The members of the Council include the Secretary of the Treasury as Chairperson of the Council, the Chair of the Federal Reserve Board, and the heads of certain other agencies. The agencies with a role in Title VIII (the CFTC, SEC, and the federal banking agencies) are all members of the Council.

Section 804 authorizes the Council to designate by at least a 2/3 vote, including the Chairperson (Secretary of the Treasury), those financial market utilities or PCS activities that the Council determines are, or are likely to become, systemically important. Prior to such determination, the Council shall consult with the relevant Supervisory Agency and the Federal Reserve Board.[89] The Council may similarly rescind a designation of systemic importance at any time.

The Council has broad authority to determine systemic importance. In addition to four listed factors, Congress provides that the Council shall consider any other factor that the Council deems appropriate. The Council must consider the following statutory factors:

- first, the aggregate monetary value of transactions processed by the utility or carried out through the PCS activity;

---

[89] By referring to the defined term "Supervisory Agency," this provision apparently does not require the Council to consult with a Federal banking regulator with respect to a financial institution that conducts a PCS activity but that is not a utility regardless of whether the PCS activity is determined to be systemically important.

- second, the aggregate exposure of the utility or financial institution to its counterparties;
- third, the relationship, interdependencies, or other interactions of the utility or PCS activity with other financial market utilities or PCS activities; and,
- fourth, the effect that the failure of or a disruption to the utility or PCS activity would have on critical markets, financial institutions, or the broader financial system.

The Council must give advance notice of the proposed determination and opportunity for a written or oral hearing before the Council to the utility or financial institution. The Council may waive or modify those procedural safeguards, however, upon 2/3 vote, including the Chairperson, if necessary to prevent or mitigate an immediate threat to the financial system posed by the utility or PCS activity. The Council's final determination must be made within 60 days of any hearing or 30 days after the expiration of the opportunity to request a hearing, and the Council may extend the time periods affecting the consultation, notice, and hearing process.

In connection with assessing systemic importance, the Council may require any utility or financial institution to submit information as the Council may require if the Council has reasonable cause to believe that the utility or PCS activity meets the standards for systemic importance.[90]

Risk Management Standards

The statutory changes made by Title VIII are consistent with the view of international banking authorities that the oversight of payment and settlement systems is a core responsibility of central banks. Except with respect to designated clearing entities, section 805 of Title VIII authorizes the Fed to prescribe risk management standards, in consultation with the Council and Supervisory Agencies, governing the operations related to PCS activities of systemically important financial market utilities and the conduct of systemically important PCS activities by financial institutions. The Fed may prescribe such standards by rule or order and must take into consideration relevant international standards and existing prudential requirements.

The CFTC and the SEC may each prescribe regulations, in consultation with the Council and the Fed, containing risk management standards of similar scope for systemically important DCOs and CAs, respectively, and supervised financial institutions (for example, a futures commission merchant supervised by the CFTC) that engage in systemically important PCS activities. Those regulations, like the Fed's standards, must take into consideration relevant international standards and existing prudential requirements.

If the Fed determines that CFTC or SEC rules are insufficient to prevent or mitigate certain risks to the financial markets or to the financial stability of the United States, the Fed may impose risk management standards on an SEC- or CFTC-regulated entity. If the CFTC or the SEC objects within 60 days of the Fed's determination, then the Council would decide with a 2/3 vote which agency's risk management standards would apply.

---

[90] Because Title VIII does not set forth standards for systemic importance, this text apparently refers to statutory considerations rather than standards.

The standards of the Fed, the CFTC, and the SEC may address areas such as risk management policies and procedures, margin and collateral requirements, participant or counterparty default policies and procedures, the ability to complete timely clearing and settlement of financial transactions, and capital and financial resource requirements for designated financial market utilities.[91] The agencies' standards must, where appropriate, establish a threshold of the amount (level or significance) of an institution's activity that will cause the standards to apply to the institution.

The Fed and the Council may not impose standards with respect to certain specified areas under CFTC or SEC authority, including the approval of clearing requirements, transaction reporting, or trade execution.[92] Further, pursuant to section 811, Title VIII in general does not divest any federal or state agency of any authority derived from any other applicable law. However, any standards prescribed by the Federal Reserve Board under section 805 shall supersede any less stringent requirements established under other authority.

Federal Reserve Services for Systemically Important Financial Market Utilities

Section 806 applies four Federal Reserve services or requirements to FMUs that apply to depository institutions. First, designated utilities may have certain accounts and deposit accounts at Federal Reserve Banks provided to depository institutions. Second, Federal Reserve Banks may pay earnings on balances maintained by a designated utility to the same extent paid to depository institutions. Third, the Fed may exempt a designated utility from reserve requirements or modify any applicable reserve requirement. Lastly, the Fed may authorize a Federal Reserve Bank to provide discount and borrowing privileges to a designated utility, but only in unusual or exigent circumstances and upon majority vote of the Fed after consultation with the Secretary of the Treasury. The utility would have to show that it is unable to secure adequate credit accommodations from other banking institutions.

Title VIII also establishes procedures that a systemically important financial market utility must follow when proposing changes to its rules, procedures, or operations. The designated utility must provide its Supervisory Agency with 60 days' advance notice of a proposed change that could materially affect the nature or level of risks presented by the utility. If the agency objects within 60 days, the utility may not implement the change. However, a designated utility may implement changes on an emergency basis in order for the utility to provide its services in a safe and sound manner.

Examination and Enforcement

Section 807 requires a Supervisory Agency to conduct examinations at least annually of a systemically important financial market utility to assess compliance with Title VIII.[93] In addition

---

[91] Congress did not authorize regulators under Title VIII to modify existing prudential capital and financial resource requirements that apply to financial institutions conducting systemically important PCS activities.

[92] The Fed's enforcement authority under Section 807(e) and (f), however, is not subject to the same limitations.

[93] A Supervisory Agency also may examine services integral to the operation of the utility by a third-party service provider.

to standard-setting authority, Congress gives the Fed a role in examinations conducted by prudential regulators and enforcement for compliance with Title VIII. The Fed may, at its discretion, participate in an examination of a systemically important utility and may exercise back-up examination authority of a financial institution in certain circumstances. Title VIII also enables the Fed to take enforcement actions directly when necessary and with the Council's approval.

The Supervisory Agency must consult with the Fed at least annually regarding the scope of such examinations. The Fed in its discretion may participate in such examinations led by the Supervisory Agency. After consulting with the Council and Supervisory Agency, the Fed may at any time recommend that the agency take enforcement action to prevent risks to the financial markets or the financial stability of the United States. In the event of imminent risk of substantial harm to financial institutions, critical markets, or the U.S. financial system, the Fed with the affirmative vote of the Council may take enforcement action against the designated utility.

Section 808 authorizes the appropriate financial regulator of a financial institution to examine such institution with respect to a systemically important PCS activity for compliance with Title VIII. The Fed may consult with, and provide technical assistance to, the appropriate financial regulator, and the regulator may ask the Fed to conduct or participate in such examination or enforce Title VIII against the financial institution. Title VIII also gives the Fed back-up examination and enforcement authority, which the Fed may exercise with the Council's approval under certain conditions, including having reasonable cause to believe that a financial institution is not in compliance with Title VIII.

Title VIII extends certain enforcement provisions of section 8 of the Federal Deposit Insurance Act[94] to a systemically important financial market utility to the same extent as if the utility were an insured depository institution and to a financial institution subject to standards for a systemically important PCS activity.

Regulatory Coordination

As described in the purposes of Title VIII in Section 802, Congress is trying to mitigate systemic risk in the financial system and promote financial stability by authorizing the Board to promote uniform risk management standards for relevant institutions. It also aims to accomplish this by providing the Board an enhanced role in the supervision of such standards. Title VIII, however, in general maintains certain regulatory and supervisory authority of the CFTC and SEC with respect to designated clearing entities. Further, Title VIII establishes various limitations requiring the Fed to consult with or act in coordination with the primary supervisor of a utility or financial institution and to obtain approval of the Council to exercise certain authority. The Council similarly must consult with or act in coordination with other agencies in certain circumstances.

Title VIII does not remove prudential oversight by federal and state regulatory and supervisory agencies of their supervised institutions. In general, the Federal Reserve must exercise its new authority and responsibilities in coordination with prudential regulators. In some circumstances, however, the Federal Reserve may take actions, or seek approval of the Financial Stability Oversight Council to take actions, without the agreement of the primary supervisory agency.

---

[94] 12 U.S.C. Section 1818(i).

The following provisions illustrate examples of required regulatory coordination under Title VIII:

- the Council must consult with the Fed and Supervisory Agencies in making systemic importance determinations under Section 804;
- the Fed or the Council must coordinate with a utility's Supervisory Agency or a financial institution's supervisor to request material information from or impose reporting or recordkeeping requirements on the entity under Section 809;
- the Fed, Council, Supervisory Agency, and appropriate financial regulator are authorized to promptly notify each other of material concerns about a designated utility or financial institution engaged in designated activities and share appropriate reports, information, or data relating to such concerns under Section 809(e); and
- coordination of examination and enforcement authority under Sections 807 and 808 is required, except to the extent that the Fed may exercise back-up or independent authority in limited circumstances.

Under Section 811, Title VIII does not divest agencies of existing authority derived from other applicable law except that standards prescribed by the Fed supersede any less stringent requirements established under other authority to the extent of a conflict.

The Conference Committee added certain provisions that limit the role of the Federal Reserve with respect to entities supervised by the CFTC and SEC. For example, Section 805 authorizes the CFTC and SEC to prescribe risk management standards for designated clearing entities (registered derivatives clearing organizations and registered clearing agencies), which the Fed can potentially override with the approval of the Council.

Title VIII also requires the CFTC and SEC to exercise certain authority in coordination with the Fed. Section 812 requires the CFTC and SEC to consult with the Fed prior to exercising authorities, including rulemaking authorities, under various provisions of law as amended by Title VIII. Section 813 requires the CFTC and the SEC to coordinate with the Fed to jointly develop risk management supervision programs for designated clearing entities.

Title VIII Implementation

Financial Stability Oversight Council

FSOC promulgated final rules for Title VIII on July 18, 2011. The rules authorized FSOC to designate financial market utilities it deemed systemically important. FSOC determines whether an FMU is systemically important if any failure of an FMUs operations could "create or increase the risk of significant liquidity or credit problems spreading among financial institutions or markets and thereby threaten the stability of the U.S. financial system."[95]

---

[95] Financial Stability Oversight Council, "Final Rules," press release, January 18, 2011, available at http://www.treasury.gov/initiatives/fsoc/Pages/final-rules.aspx.

Federal Reserve

Section 805 of the Dodd-Frank Act provides that, except for certain entities supervised by the CFTC and SEC, the Federal Reserve by rule or order shall prescribe risk management standards governing operations of systemically important utilities and the conduct of systemically important activities by financial institutions. On July 30, 2012, The Federal Reserve released its final rule regarding FMUs. It comprises much of the same material that was included in the proposed rules. The final rule implements risk management standards for FMUs, and standards for determining when FMUs must give notice about changes to rules, procedures, or operations that would alter the nature of risks they present. The addition of two rules, one centering on application waivers, and the other revising the list of changes that do not require notice, mark the difference between the final rule and the proposed rule.[96]

CFTC and SEC

Title VIII provides the CFTC and the SEC, respectively, with additional authority to supervise and regulate those systemically important utilities that are derivatives clearing organizations (DCOs) and clearing agencies (CAs), which together are called designated clearing entities.

Section 805 of the Dodd-Frank Act authorizes the CFTC and SEC to prescribe regulations containing risk management standards governing the operations of designated clearing entities or the conduct of designated activities by financial institutions that each agency supervises. Although the Fed may challenge such rules as insufficient, the CFTC and SEC may object to the Council regarding the Fed's determination. The Council would make the final decision upon the affirmative 2/3 vote of its members.

In July 2011, the Fed, CFTC, and SEC outlined the rulemaking governing their new authorities over DCOs and CAs, detailing the enhanced risk management standards these entities must follow.[97] That rulemaking has since been largely finalized. For instance, the SEC announced final rules on June 28, 2012 specifying registering and review procedures for CAs.[98] The CFTC announced a final rule on April 9, 2012, adopting new Dodd-Frank statutory provisions.[99]

The scope of Title VIII encompasses the infrastructure for the clearing of OTC derivatives, which is governed by the regulatory framework established in Title VII of the Dodd-Frank Act. Title VII requires firms to clear certain OTC derivatives, including credit default swaps, through central counterparties. Both the CFTC and the SEC must write various rules to implement Title VII, which will apply to derivatives clearing organizations and clearing agencies supervised by those agencies.[100] The clearing requirements in Title VII could increase the likelihood of a systemic

---

[96] Board of Governors of the Federal Reserve System, *Financial Market Utilities*, RIN No. 7100-AD 71, July 30, 2012, available at http://www.theclearinghouse.org/index.html?f=074147.

[97] Board of Governors of the Federal Reserve, Securities and Exchange Commission, and Commodity Futures Trading Commission, *Risk Management Supervision of Designated Clearing Entities*, Securities and Exchange Commission, Washington, D.C., July 2011, p. 3, available at http://www.sec.gov/news/studies/2011/813study.pdf.

[98] Available at http://www.sec.gov/rules/final/2012/34-67286.pdf.

[99] Available at http://www.cftc.gov/ucm/groups/public/@lrfederalregister/documents/file/2012-7477a.pdf.

[100] International standards applicable to clearing organizations have also undergone revision. See, Committee on Payment and Settlement Systems, *Principles for Financial* (continued...)

importance designation under Title VIII for financial market utilities that engage in clearing OTC derivatives.

Impact on Payment, Clearing, and Settlement Systems and Activities

Those financial market utilities and PCS activities conducted by financial institutions that are designated as systemically important will be affected by additional supervision and requirements to comply with newly adopted risk management and conduct standards. Further, those designated firms could potentially be subject to increased oversight through the Federal Reserve's enhanced examination authority and role in enforcing compliance with applicable rules.

Certain payment system infrastructures were previously subject to Federal Reserve or other agency oversight. Newer systems and technologies may be developed in the future to process financial transactions via the Internet and by other means. The impact on evolving technologies would depend upon the extent to which their activities fall within the scope of the supervisory framework established under the Dodd-Frank Act and whether newer systems become systemically important.

The impact of Title VIII on a particular entity is likely to vary depending upon whether a financial market utility or financial institution is currently subject to Federal Reserve supervision, whether a system or institution has operated previously outside the scope of bank regulatory or other federal agency oversight, and whether the utility or institution will also be subject to requirements and potentially increased clearing transaction volume under Title VII requirements.

The impact of Title VIII will also depend upon the actions of various regulators such as how broadly the Financial Stability Oversight Council applies the designation of systemic importance to financial market utilities and PCS activities of financial institutions and how stringently the Fed, CFTC and SEC decide to set risk management rules and standards.

(...continued)

Market Infrastructures, Bank for International Settlements, Basel, Switzerland, April 1, 2012, http://www.bis.org/publ/cpss101a.pdf. In May 2010, the CPSS and IOSCO released guidance with respect to how the 2004 Recommendations for central counterparties should be applied to the handling of OTC derivatives by central counterparties. Bank for International Settlements, Committee on Payment and Settlement Systems, *Guidance on the Application of the 2004 CPSS-IOSCO Recommendations for Central Counterparties to OTC Derivatives CCPs – Consultative Report*, CPSS Publications No. 89, Basel, Switzerland, May 2010, http://www.bis.org/publ/cpss89.pdf. In November 2010, the CPSS released a report entitled, *Market Structure Developments in the Clearing Industry: Implications for Financial Stability.* Bank for International Settlements, Committee on Payment and Settlement Systems, CPSS Publications No. 92, Basel, Switzerland, http://www.bis.org/publ/cpss92.pdf.

Appendix. Selected Payment, Clearing, and Settlement Systems in the United States

Table A-1. Selected FMUs Designated Systematically Important by FSOC

The Depository Trust Company	Central securities depository. DTC is a member of the Federal Reserve System, a limited-purpose trust company under New York State banking law supervised by the New York State Banking Department, and a registered clearing agency with the SEC.	The Depository Trust & Clearing Corporation (DTCC). DTCC is owned by its users, including major banks, broker-dealers, and other financial institutions.	Banks and broker-dealers. In 2008, there were 413 participants.	Settling trades in corporate, municipal, and mortgage-backed securities.	DTC moves securities for net settlements of the NSCC, which is also owned by DTCC, and settlement for institutional trades typically involving money and securities transfers between custodian banks and broker-dealers as well as money market instruments.	In 2011, processed 302.3 million transactions, a 2.0% increase from 2010, valued at $1.669 quadrillion. The average value per transaction was $5.5 million.
National Securities Clearing Corporation (NSCC)	Regulated by the SEC	DTCC, which is owned by its users, including major banks, broker-dealers, and other financial institutions.	Brokers. In 2008, there were 221 participants.	Clearing, settlement, and central counterparty services for virtually all broker-to-broker trades in the U.S. involving equities and corporate and municipal debt.		In 2011, cleared 20.8 billion transactions, a 2.0% increase from 2010, valued at $220.9 trillion. The average value per transaction was $10.5 thousand.

Entity	Regulation	Ownership	Participants	Services	Transactions	Statistics
Fixed Income Clearing Corporation (FICC)	Registered with and regulated by the SEC. Operates two divisions, the Government Securities Division (GSD) and the Mortgage-Backed Securities Division (MBSD). Each division offers services to their own members pursuant to separate rules and procedures.	DTCC, which is owned by its users, including major banks, broker-dealers, and other financial institutions.	GSD: broker-dealers, banks, and other financial institutions trading in the U.S. government-securities marketplace. In 2008, there were 97 participants in the GSD. MBSD: participants include mortgage originators, government-sponsored enterprises, broker-dealers, banks, and other financial institutions. In 2008, there were 103 participants in the MBSD.	GSD is a central counterparty and provides real-time trade matching, netting, and clearing services for trades in U.S. government debt issues, including repurchase (repo) agreements. MBSD provides real-time trade matching, netting, and clearing services for the mortgage-backed securities market.	Securities transactions processed by GSD include Treasury bills, bonds, notes, and government agency securities.	In 2011, GSD cleared 40.5 million transactions, a 19% increase from 2010, valued at $1.13 quadrillion. The average value per transaction was $27.9 million. In 2011, MBSD cleared 3.9 million transactions, a 22% increase from 2010, valued at $97.7 trillion. The average value per transaction was $25 million.
The Clearing House Payments Company	Payment, clearing and settlement operator. Operates CHIPS, EPN, and SVPCO Image. Regulated by the Federal Reserve.	Owned by Member banks and financial institutions. Member banks are among the largest banks in the world.	Provides payment, clearing, and settlement services to member banks and financial institutions.	Under CHIPS, provides payment, clearing, and settlement services in real time using U.S. dollars. Under EPN, operates private ACH services. And under SVPCO Image Exchange, provides settlement and reporting of digital images of paper checks.	Chips processes wire transfer payments for banks. EPN handles payroll, dividends, and other types of credit transfers. SVPCO Image, provides check images throughout a network of financial institutions.	The value of CHIPS transactions in 2011 amounted to $403.3 trillion. That same year, the average daily dollar amount exceeded $1.6 trillion. 52 banks participated with a total of 95 thousand transactions.

Chicago Mercantile Exchange	Futures trading industry regulated by the Federal Reserve.	Owned by the CME Group, which provides the largest options and futures products of any exchange in the world. CME Group is comprised of NYMEX, CBOT, COMEX, and CME.	Traders and investors in options and futures contracts who are members of the CME.	An exchange that allows members to trade products and to trade directly on trading floor.	Principal transactions are trading various types of derivative products like futures and options.	In August 2012, the average volume was 91 million for futures and 15 million for options.
The Options Clearing Corporation	Operates under the jurisdiction of both the CFTC (registered DCO) and the SEC.	Founded in 1973, is the world's largest DCO. The stockholder exchanges share equal ownership of the OCC.	Approximately 130 of the largest U.S. broker-dealers, U.S. futures commission merchants, and non-U.S. securities firms representing professional traders and public customers.	Serves role as guarantor and central counterparty. Daily settlement of U.S. dollar payments is effected through a network of money-center banks.	Under SEC jurisdiction, clears transactions for options and security futures. As DCO, provides clearing and settlement services for transactions in futures and options on futures.	In 2011, processed 4.5 billion options contracts (daily average of 18.1 million) and 38.2 million futures contracts (daily average 151 thousand)
ICE Trust	Limited purpose New York trust company (New York State Banking Department). Member of the Federal Reserve System. Operates under an exemption from the SEC and the U.S. Treasury Department.	Operated by Intercontinental Exchange, a publicly listed company, which operates three regulated futures exchanges, trading platforms, clearinghouses, and over-the-counter markets.	14 clearing firm members. Customers of ICE are commercial hedgers, traders, brokers, risk managers, futures commission merchants, and portfolio managers.	Central credit facility for credit default swaps (CDS). Began clearing CDS contracts in March 2009.	Offers CDS clearing for 89 single-name and 38 index contracts.	Between March 2009 and August 2012, cleared approximately 267 thousand corporate and sovereign single-name CDS trades (with a gross notional cleared value of $1.835 trillion) and 240 thousand index CDS trades (with a gross notional cleared value of $17.4 trillion).

CLS Bank	Multi-currency cash settlement system founded in 1997	Financial services institutions in the foreign exchange business.	Settlement members and user members.	Settles payment instructions related to trades executed in six traded instruments and in 17 major currencies. Eliminates risk associated with foreign exchange settlement across time zones.	Foreign exchange	Settles 55% of the world's foreign exchange payment instructions (as of August 2012,)

Source: CPSS Publication No 88, Red Book Statistical Update, Statistics on payment and settlement systems in selected countries, December 2009, available at http://www.bis.org/publ/cpss88.htm; U.S. Department of the Treasury, Blueprint for a Modernized Financial Regulatory Structure, March 2008; Federal Reserve website at http://www.federalreserve.gov/paymentsystems/fedfunds_data.htm, and http://www.federalreserve.gov/paymentsystems/fedsecs_data.htm; Volume/Value data acquired from websites of selected systems each accessed in August 2012.Click here and type the source, or delete this paragraph

Table A-2. Other PCS Systems

Name	Type/Regulator	Owners/Operators	Users/Participants	Uses/Functions	Transactions	Volume/Value
Fedwire Funds Service	Real-time gross settlement system (RGSS). Payments are continuously settled on an individual, order-by-order basis without netting. Transfer of funds is final and irrevocable when settled.	Federal Reserve/Federal Reserve Banks	Depository institutions, U.S. Treasury, Federal government agencies. In 2008, there were 5,458 participants (excluding the U.S. Treasury and certain other domestic and foreign entities), a decrease from the 6,388 participants in 2007.	Sending funds to other institutions, including for customers. Payment orders by depository institutions are processed individually and settled in central bank money upon receipt. The U.S. Treasury and other federal agencies use this service to disburse and receive funds.	Purchase and sale of federal funds (depository institutions lend balances at the Federal Reserve to other depository institutions overnight); purchase, sale, and financing of securities transactions; disbursement or repayment of loans; settlement of cross-border U.S. dollar commercial transactions; settlement of real estate transactions and other high-value, time-critical payments.	In 2011, there were 127 million transfers originated (a 1.5% increase from 2010), valued at $663 trillion. The average value per transfer was $5.23 million. In 2012 (Q1), the average daily volume of transfers (for business days) was 514 thousand with an average daily value of $2.35 trillion.

Name	Type/Regulator	Owners/Operators	Users/Participants	Uses/Functions	Transactions	Volume/Value
Fedwire Securities Service (National Book-Entry System)	Real-time transfers on individual or gross basis. Transfer of securities and related funds, if any, is final and irrevocable when made. Most securities transfers involve the simultaneous exchange of payment known as delivery versus payment (DVP), which ensures that the final transfer of securities occurs if and only if the final transfer of payment occurs.	Federal Reserve/Federal Reserve Banks. The Federal Reserve Banks act as fiscal agents to facilitate the issuance of book-entry securities to participants.	Limited to depository institutions and a few other entities, including the U.S. Treasury, government-sponsored enterprises, state treasurers, and limited-purpose trust companies that are members of the Federal Reserve System. Nonbank broker-dealers typically hold and transfer their Fedwire securities through depository institution participants. In 2008, there were 1,203 participants in NBES.	Issuance, transfer, and settlement for all marketable Treasury securities, for many federal government agency and government-sponsored enterprise securities, and for certain international organizations' securities. There is a safekeeping function (electronic storage of securities holding records in custody accounts) and a transfer and settlement function (electronic transfer of securities between parties with or without a settlement payment).	Transfer of securities — for example, to settle secondary market trades, including open market operations; to move collateral used to secure obligations; and to facilitate repurchase (repo) agreement transactions.	In 2011, there were 18.6 million transfers originated (a 5.9% decrease from 2010), valued at $291.8 trillion. The average value per transfer was $15.6 million. In 2012 (Q1), the average daily volume of transfers (for business days) was 74.6 thousand with an average daily value of $1.1 trillion. Securities held in custody at end of 2nd quarter 2010 were $61 trillion.
National Settlement Service (NSS)	Multilateral settlement service implemented in March 1999. Settlement finality occurs on day of settlement.	Federal Reserve/Federal Reserve Banks	Depository institutions that settle for participants in clearinghouses, financial exchanges, and other clearing and settlement groups. Key private-sector system users include DTC and NSCC for end-of-day cash settlement; FICC for funds-only settlement; EPN; The Options Clearing Corp; and several large and regional check clearinghouses.	Settlement agents acting on behalf of depository institution participants in a settlement arrangement electronically submit settlement files to the Federal Reserve Banks. The files are processed upon receipt, and entries are automatically posted to a depository institution's Federal Reserve account.	Currently, there are approximately 40 NSS arrangements establishes by financial market utilities, check clearinghouse associations, and automated clearinghouse networks.	In 2011, processed about 571,000 transfers valued at about $15.7 trillion. In 2012 (Q1), the average daily volume of entries processed was 2,585 with an average daily settlement value of $63.75 billion.

Name	Type/Regulator	Owners/Operators	Users/Participants	Uses/Functions	Transactions	Volume/Value
FedACH Service	Electronic payment system providing automated clearing house (ACH) services.	Federal Reserve/Federal Reserve Banks	Depository institutions	The ACH system exchanges batched debit and credit payments among business, consumer, and government accounts.	Pre-authorized recurring payments such as payroll, Social Security, mortgage, and utility payments. Non-recurring payments such as telephone-initiated payments and the conversion of checks into ACH payments at lockboxes and points of sale. Also outbound cross-border ACH payments through FedGlobal service.	In 2009, originated 13.4 billion transactions with a value of $22.3 trillion.
Electronic Payments Network (EPN)	ACH operator	The Clearing House, which is owned by the largest U.S. banks or the U.S. branches or affiliates of major foreign banks.	Over 1350 financial institutions. Approximately 53% of customers are credit unions, 36% commercial, 9% savings, and 2% savings and loan institutions.	Payment system handling credit transfers such as payroll and dividends and debit transfers such as loan and bill payments and insurance premiums.	Processes 48% of all commercial ACH volume in the U.S.	Processes over 6.5 billion transactions annually.
Society for Worldwide Interbank Financial Telecommunication (SWIFT)	Financial messaging service	User-owned, limited liability cooperative organized under Belgian law headquartered in Belgium with operational centers in the Netherlands and the United States.	More than 9,000 banking organizations, securities institutions, and corporate customers in 209 countries. U.S. financial intermediaries are among the heaviest users of SWIFT services for correspondent banking communications.	Provides secure, standardized financial messages and related services to its member financial institutions, their market infrastructures, and their end-users.		As of June 2012, processed 2.3 billion messages year-to-date, averaging 18.2 million messages per business day.

List of Acronyms of Selected Terms

ACH	Automated clearing house
ANPR	Advance Notice of Proposed Rulemaking
BIS	Bank for International Settlements
CA	Clearing agency
CCP	Central counterparty
CDS	Credit default swap
CFTC	U.S. Commodity Futures Trading Commission
Council	Financial Stability Oversight Council
CPSS	Committee on Payment and Settlement Systems
DCO	Derivatives clearing organization
Dodd-Frank Act	Dodd-Frank Wall Street Reform and Consumer Protection Act
EFT	Electronic funds transfer
FFIEC	Federal Financial Institutions Examination Council
Fed	Federal Reserve System
FI	Financial institution
FMU	Financial market utility
FSA	United Kingdom Financial Services Authority
IOSCO	International Organization of Securities Commissions
MOU	Memorandum of Understanding
OTC	Over-the-counter
PCS	Payment, clearing, and settlement
PSR Policy	Federal Reserve Policy on Payment System Risk
Repo	Repurchase agreement
RTGS	Real-time gross settlement
SEC	U.S. Securities and Exchange Commission
Title VII	Wall Street Transparency and Accountability Act of 2010
Title VIII	Payment, Clearing, and Settlement Supervision Act of 2010

Author Contact Information

Marc Labonte
Specialist in Macroeconomic Policy
mlabonte@crs.loc.gov, 7-0640

Acknowledgments

This report was originally written by Donna Nordenberg, who is no longer with CRS. This report was updated by Victor Tineo, Presidential Management Fellow.

www.ingramcontent.com/pod-product-compliance
Lightning Source LLC
Chambersburg PA
CBHW081245180526
45171CB00005B/544